Published by The Child's World®
1980 Lookout Drive • Mankato, MN 56003-1705
800-599-READ • www.childsworld.com

Photographs ©: Yuri Arcurs/iStockphoto, cover (fairy), 1 (fairy); Julia Ardaran/Shutterstock Images, cover (background), 1–3 (background), 6, 24; Shutterstock Images, 5, 14, 15, 16, 17, 18, 23; Gianni Marchetti/Shutterstock Images, 9; iStockphoto, 10, 13; Glenn Hill/SSPL/Getty Images, 11; S. Bukley/Shutterstock Images, 19; Dmitry Morgan/Shutterstock Images, 20; Atelier Sommerland/Shutterstock Images, 21

Copyright © 2022 by The Child's World®
All rights reserved. No part of this book may be reproduced or utilized in any form or by any means without written permission from the publisher.

ISBN 9781503849761 (Reinforced Library Binding)
ISBN 9781503850774 (Portable Document Format)
ISBN 9781503851535 (Online Multi-user eBook)
LCCN 2021939348

Printed in the United States of America

Table of CONTENTS

CHAPTER ONE

Inside a Fairy Circle…4

CHAPTER TWO

History of Fairies…8

CHAPTER THREE

Wings and Magic…12

CHAPTER FOUR

Fairies Today…18

Glossary…22

To Learn More…23

Index…24

CHAPTER ONE

INSIDE A FAIRY CIRCLE

Ella went outside to play in the yard. She noticed a ring of dark green grass. When she went to play the next week, there were mushrooms, too. They made a circle in the yard.

Her mother told her the rings were called fairy circles. Stories said that the circles were doors to the land of the fairies. Some stories said it was dangerous to enter fairy land. People would be forced to dance with the fairies. They would not be able to stop, even if they got tired. Other stories said time passed differently in fairy land. A few minutes there could be weeks in the human world. Stories said people who went to the land of the fairies often did not come back.

Fairy circles can be caused by mushrooms.

In many stories, people who enter the land of fairies do not return to the human world.

Ella knew fairies were not real. But she thought it would be exciting if they were. She went out to the backyard. Ella stood on the edge of the fairy circle. She wanted to leap into the center of it. But Ella was a little worried. What if she got lost in fairy land? Ella took a deep breath. She shut her eyes. She jumped over the ring of mushrooms. The grass felt soft under her feet. She opened her eyes. Ella was still at home. The fairy circle was just a circle of mushrooms. It would not take her anywhere.

Fairies are legendary creatures. Stories of fairylike creatures exist around the world. People have told stories about fairies for thousands of years. Some say fairies are helpful. Other stories say that fairies play tricks. But stories of fairies have inspired many people. People look for fairies. They make up new stories about them.

CHAPTER TWO
HISTORY OF FAIRIES

Fairy stories exist around the world. They come from every continent except Antarctica. Some of these legends are thousands of years old.

Several native peoples around the world tell stories of fairies. Tupi-Guarani speaking peoples in Brazil describe fairies that live in the forest. In Australia, the Arunta people tell stories of an invisible fairy. In North America, the Inuit, Cherokee, Iroquois, and Abenaki peoples all have legends of fairylike creatures. Each culture calls these creatures something different. But some parts of each story are similar. The stories say most fairylike creatures are small. They live in the water or forest.

Anhangá is a fairy described by the Tupi people. The fairy takes the form of a white deer with red eyes. It protects animals.

Folklore from Ireland and Scotland describes fairies many people recognize today. In Ireland, some people say it's bad luck to say the word *fairy* out loud. People believe fairies can hear the word and then play tricks on the person who said it. Instead, people say other words or phrases to describe fairies. These include *little people* or *fair folk*.

The Cottingley Fairies hoax was created by two young cousins in 1917. They admitted their fairy photos were fake in 1983.

Stories say the creatures are magical. People looked for them. Some people claimed they saw fairies. Sightings of fairies continued into the 1900s. Some people even made fake pictures of fairies. They said the pictures were **evidence** that fairies existed. But these pictures were **hoaxes**. No one has ever photographed a fairy.

CHAPTER THREE

WINGS AND MAGIC

Many legends about fairies are similar. Fairies are magical. They often look like humans, but they are more beautiful. Fairies can choose to be helpful or harmful. Many stories say fairies make beautiful music.

Leprechauns are a type of fairy. Stories about them come from Ireland. Leprechauns are **tricksters**. They can disappear suddenly.

wings

pointed ears

human face

small size

Most stories say fairies look like humans. But a fairy's wings and magical powers set it apart from humans.

People from Scotland tell stories about brownies. These fairies are often helpful. They clean homes for people at night when everyone is asleep. People leave milk, cream, or bread out for the brownies to say thank you.

Stories say that brownies are easily offended. If a human leaves a gift the brownie does not like, the brownie will disappear and never help again.

Stories of fairies and fairylike creatures exist around the world.

In Inuit culture, one kind of fairy lives under the ice. People give **offerings** to the fairies. Stories say fairies lead hunters to seals and fish.

Some stories say fairies are very small. A fairy can fit inside a flower.

Many stories say fairies have pointed ears like elves. Legends say fairies can be different sizes. Some fairies are the same size as humans. Other stories describe fairies as only a few inches tall.

Some types of fairies can fly. Many drawings show fairies with butterfly or dragonfly wings. But other types of fairies cannot fly. Brownies and leprechauns are two examples.

Though leprechauns are a type of fairy, they can't fly.

CHAPTER FOUR
FAIRIES TODAY

People continue to create stories about fairies. Stories are a little different today than they were hundreds of years ago. Most stories today show fairies as helpful. Fewer stories show fairies as **mischievous**. Almost all modern fairy stories show them with wings and brightly colored clothing. In older stories, a fairy's clothing blended in with the landscape.

Rosetta, Silvermist, Tinker Bell, Iridessa, and Fawn are some of the Disney Fairies from the Tinker Bell movies.

Today's stories say these creatures are small. For example, Tinker Bell from *Peter Pan* fits in the palm of Peter's hand. She flies quickly from place to place. Artists at Disney made more movies about Tinker Bell. These movies are about Tinker Bell and her fairy friends.

Sleeping Beauty *features good fairies and evil fairies.*

Some fairy stories today are similar to each other. Fairies often live in or near forests. For example, the three fairies in *Sleeping Beauty* raise Aurora in a cottage in the woods. Fairies in stories usually have wings.

Fairies also have magical powers. In *Peter Pan*, Tinker Bell uses fairy dust to help people fly. In *Sleeping Beauty*, the fairies use magic to make cakes and dresses. Even though fairies do not exist in real life, people continue to make new stories. Each one adds a new twist to the list of stories about fairies.

Fairy stories continue to enchant people.

GLOSSARY

evidence (EH-vuh-dunss) Evidence is a piece of information that helps researchers understand a question. People used photos as evidence that fairies were real.

folklore (FOHK-lor) Folklore is the stories and beliefs that a group of people have passed down through the generations. Scottish and Irish folklore includes fairies.

hoaxes (HOHKSS-es) Hoaxes are events or objects that have been faked. Photos of fairies turned out to be hoaxes.

mischievous (MISS-chuv-vuhss) Someone who is mischievous behaves in an annoying or slightly harmful way. In many older fairy stories, fairies were mischievous rather than kind or helpful.

offerings (AH-fur-ingz) Offerings are gifts left for someone, often a supernatural being. In some cultures, people leave offerings for fairies.

tricksters (TRIK-stuhrs) Tricksters are people or creatures that play tricks on other people on purpose. Leprechauns are tricksters.

TO LEARN MORE

In the Library

Morlock, Theresa. *Fairy and Leprechaun Legends*. New York, NY: Gareth Stevens Publishing, 2018.

Nobleman, Marc Tyler. *Fairy Spell: How Two Girls Convinced the World that Fairies Are Real*. New York, NY: Clarion Books, 2018.

Qitsualik-Tinsley, Rachel and Sean. *How Things Came to Be: Inuit Stories of Creation*. Nunavut, Canada: Inhabit Media, 2015.

On the Web

Visit our website for links about fairies:

childsworld.com/links

Note to Parents, Teachers, and Librarians: We routinely verify our Web links to make sure they are safe and active sites. So encourage your readers to check them out!

INDEX

appearance, 8, 12, 17, 18–20

brownies, 14, 17

fairy circles, 4–7

hoaxes, 11

leprechauns, 12, 17

music, 4, 12

powers, 4, 10–11, 12–15, 21

Sleeping Beauty, 20–21

Tinker Bell, 19, 21

wings, 17, 18–20

ABOUT THE AUTHOR

Marty Erickson is a writer living in Minnesota. They write books for young people full time and like to go hiking.